SH
EE
TS

SHEETS

TYPEWRITER WORKS

Cameron Anstee

Invisible Publishing
Halifax & Toronto

Library and Archives Canada Cataloguing in Publication

Title: Sheets : typewriter works / Cameron Anstee.
Names: Anstee, Cameron, author.
Description: Poems.
Identifiers: Canadiana 20220394539 | ISBN 9781778430084 (softcover)
Classification: LCC PS8601.N555 S54 2022 | DDC C811/.6—dc23

Edited by derek beaulieu
Cover and interior design by Megan Fildes
With thanks to type designer Rod McDonald

Invisible Publishing is committed to protecting our natural environment. As part of our efforts, both the cover and interior of this book are printed on acid-free 100% post-consumer recycled fibres.

Printed and bound in Canada

Invisible Publishing | Halifax & Toronto
www.invisiblepublishing.com

We acknowledge for their financial support of our publishing program the Canada Council for the Arts, the Ontario Arts Council, and the Government of Canada.

CONTENTS

NOTES

pages and pages

    brief things

            --Larry Eigner

THE MOST DIFFICULT PART ABOUT TYPING
IS GETTING THE PAPER IN STRAIGHT

--Barbara Caruso

REHEARSAL

once

and once
again

once
and once
again

once
and once
again

once
and once
again

once and
and once
again

and once

and once

again

AFTERWORKS I

Ellipsis (Lowercase)

AFTER HEIDI NEILSON

The Golden Ratio

AFTER PSW

I.

II.

Three Raindrops

AFTER MARY ELLEN SOLT

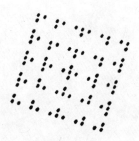

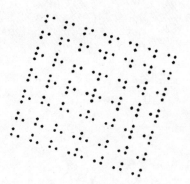

Sheets

AFTER JIŘÍ VALOCH

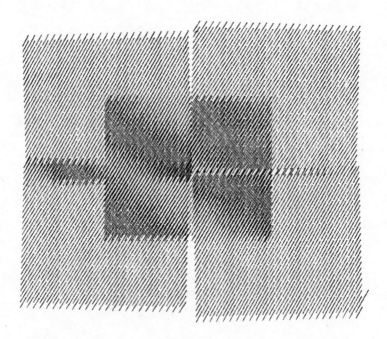

Evening Spring Sound

AFTER MICHAEL CASTEELS

```
wind
wind
owwo
odpe
cker
```

An Installation

AFTER ALEX PORCO

```
& sky & and &
sky & and & sky
& and & sky &
and & sky & and
```

The Great Galaxy

AFTER RUFINO TAMAYO

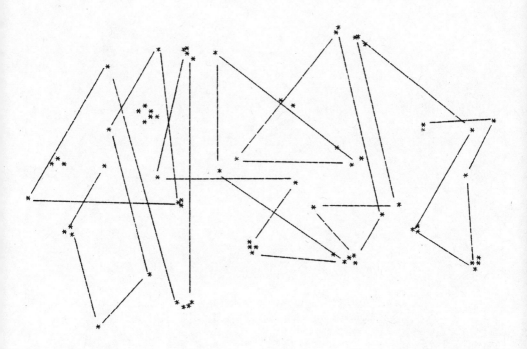

Haiku
AFTER LEROY GORMAN

silence
silence
silence

Ellipsis (Uppercase)

AFTER HEIDI NEILSON

ST. ANDREW VOICES

I'm glad I'm
home it's wide
out there   .

                --Eileen Myles

impatient birds year after year

listening to the neighbour watching the neighbour run

on the stairs footsteps the cat in the window the jasmine a wasp the pages turning the noise of the book in your hands

idle sky still there all we have ever said

out loud remembering our other memories

begun in the shade I read Larry Eigner now in the sun

lawnmower garbage can dishwasher typewriter airplane

leaf on wind on leaf on leaf

moving some sunlight or the rain or the tree or the gravel

the cats listen to the radio while we garden

rain on the winaows April open again

Sunday enclosed with the sparrows the purposeless evening

in silence the silence ajar

OTTAWA POEMS

#1

toward a starry often
a dream in my head, some trip on power
its always returning to, towards
a realization of the dilemma
the pretension of definition

these actual lines of
a kiss from it to you
(the forming farce)

standing before you
his words for its the city,
the funny many

Subject & object
buggering each other.

#2

To Indians
canoeing the Ottawa
a bleak eighty of rock
& tangled shrubbery
a nightmare of growth
climbing to the mountainsy

today tourists flock
to peer down

& some
still see Indians
canoeing the Ottawa
dipping the bleak eighty of rock
& saying no thanksxx

they they paddle on.

#3

THE FUNNY KIND OF PROPHET SPEAKS

Fucking my dear you observe
yourself fucking me
not me fucking you nor we fucking we

Or involve yourself with life
through that strange motion
& not so strange rhythm--
like the poems in all our heads never written
& that rhythm is past
present & hopefully the future
is involved in our creation
prepares or trains us for death

When the Heavenly Riots starts
(the script reads) cities will
explode from the massive rhythm
of us all
trying to get one more into
ourselves each other.

#4

What had shey Queen Victoriay in mind
naming this placey Ottawa, capital?

     Ah coolnessy he saidy
     who aug coolnessx

This crazy riverxabounding town
where people are quietly
following some hesitant
form of evolution
arranged on television
from Torontoy

Where girls are all
possible fucks
in the long dull summernights

& Mountiex more image
than reality.

48

#5

how can I describe the anger
a killing lust overcomes me with
or try how try justify
hatred of fellow man?

just one of those
impossible but frequent
happeningsxxx

I want to toughen
my attitudes
on mediocrity

& make a few statements
on values
to the crowded bastards

I reaching stop
& get afff..silent
& frightened by visions
of mad house brockville
& me in real tearsx inside.

words the song of birds
insists my bird words
the song is bird's words***
the words of birds.

outside they sing
(jesus christ I know) words of
the birds, but not of words, not of them,
the words just***

outside they are singing
those bird words.

#7

A XXXX XXXXXX XX XXXXXXXXX

Things disappear xxxxx
xxx xxxxx Xxx xxxxxx
xx xxxxxxx xxxx xx xxxx
xx X xxxxxxxx xxxxx
xx xxx xxxxxxx xxx xx xxxxxx xxxxxxxx
xxxx xxxx xxxxx
& xxxx xxxxxxx

Xxxxxxxxxx xxx xxxx
xx xxxx xxxxxxxxx
xxxx xxx xxxxxxx

& X xxxxx xxxx
what I can say
about xx lack xx xxxxxxx

& the xxxxxxxx
too immense,
xxxxxxx xx one more ending,
but xx xxxx xx which way
to begin.

#8

POEM IN RED INK

Having formed
over time   an
attitude of mistrust

plus an intimate
infatuation
with my own continued existency

I desire rest
& think bed

go to mine
for sleep

#9

A STUPID CANASTA POEM
                    **for Saunders

Make yourself above the images
of beauty keep clear
of any such attempt at permanencey

Go down on the images
you barely recall desire

as someone shutting
the bright light off

& the the ladies may twitter
at offers of head
at least your own goings are in perfect bliss
trying to fill
an intellectual inside straighty knowing
that losing doesn't change much of anything
if you don't take the game too seriously.

#10

Hey there don't
got a tragedy is shaping
inside my head

    & there's a fire somewhere burning

    a man's dreams
    I am told
    just down the street
    burning.

Tragic the death of dreams,
memories of Atlantis,
the symbols transformed to myth,
lying away under the couch,
in Heaven, light streaming from it,
we often don't see.

Some kind of new Viper
is playing drums

as the day finally ends.

54

#11

Your hair electric, on legs &
traces on breasty skin toney
sly ripples of pleasurey
distant explosions
in my ear & always
a burning within
& me lost in my own confusionsy

You see I am not inclined
to discretiony
can offer only
obvious love
to all beautiful people--
at night your silence
keeps me awake.

#12

The city extends
no hand to make
leaves me her

The frogs I hear are
croaking for something, some meaning,
because I catch their desires

I am a catcher of desires,
I have been alone
& now have calliance of the self.

Because of that, the loneliness,
having no one to speak to++
sitting containing
the desire++I send love to all,
screaming it, while the
actual voices begin
a pattern of fear
in ever narrowing circles.

#13

So much of me is not
beautiful so muchxxx
my grammar for instance
& I don't know the value
of my wordsx
constantlyx you saidx pouring from my head

        & thexx the words,
        are maybe patternsx from dreamsx
        from my deep sleepx

I wish you could know me
on some morningsx insidx some momentsx
& I flash my twenty-five years
on a pretentious fixe second pagx
like so & am completex

Torturesx I saidx
by our potential
to realize beautyx
within & without.

57

#14

Ruaaryy tha amxll aquarey
arxarea in ity a thraeryaarxaia bayy
strangely nine (both resent it)
coaxing some unheard of melody
from his harmonica

Iy aistraatea beingy
cannot get in tune
but will not let my ego
make judgements
any longery forced acceptance
of song everywhere
I sing & say
so thatis x & harmonica

& the kid blows a riff
out of his lonely souly turns me to glassy
me & all my pretensions about meaning.

#15

ah shit don't shout I'll sing

I sing:
        Ottawa,
        rivers & jokey
        fantasies
        the dawn don't
        slow up.

I sing:
        for songs
        Ottawa,
        you know nothing
        of poems
        & you are poems.

I sing:
        buses & poisons,
        actual criminal exhausts,
        people are falling
        victim to their conveniences

        the man
        vibrated to death
        by an electric toothbrush,

        & me
        don't I take drugs?

Listen Ottawa, I can't sleep

                seem to have forgotten
                the ancient art,

        expect too much—
        the grey truth of
        dawn now happening,
        gives incentives
        but it's too late.

Can't you tell me a story?
Put me into one more day?

59

#16

XBEAUTY WILL NOT WAITXx

will not pause
the I must name its beauty
its array will not wait
for the namer to compose
himself

        as the river
        will not, nor
        birds on their
        particular branches,

nor my memory of China
wait.

You see the sun flames up
forcing the concerns of day
upon me & upon this night
I've spent with old masters
for everyone's new questions**
the rays of light
announce themselves
& simultaneously
the hammering transcription begins,
the unpoetic aspect of breath begins.

*Charles Olson

#17

loxxx classic form six to please

        ejaculations, how many
        did it take to build
        the Rideau Canaly
        how many Saturday night two dollar bangs?

Listen I'll ask the bus driver
this very morning
how oftenxxx

        we must have
        some norxy some understanding.

Listen, don't fuck did
      because of love, gikkness
      or casual fucking is tiresomex

Listen, one day I'm going,
      someone will come & take me awayx
      For smoking shit or pissing on the
      War Memorial, for something
      they will come & take mex

What's to say we don't love them
& their cruel ways?

#18

I ~~xxxxxx xx xxxxxx~~
~~xxxx xxx~~

Grammar ~~lessons~~
~~on a river bank~~
~~he~~ gives grammar
instead of beauty

      ~~knows nothing~~
      ~~about zithers~~

~~The~~ beauty remains,
~~they will make ite~~
~~only key strange iy~~
~~then unrelated pronouny~~
~~leaves**~~

     ~~see him~~ waving ~~goodbye~~.

#19

HOMAGE TO BATMAN

Suddenly there were seams
in my mind

        I seemed to hear
        Batman

feel the axis of his climax

Remembering forgotten stars,
distant nights,
playing the Jokers crazy & dangerous game

Something about the failure of past rhythms
arising new tunes out of my head.

THE LAST POEM FOR PEOPLE

The heart speaks (to ear, ear to mouth
& mouth to brain) & the brain
seeks an answer**

(in my bitterness
I offer:

if it is your wish
to be clever as if to entertain
or to ask that
to flight
or flowery as in soul
facing

or without ambition
to rehearse & propagate & to construct
within a group of despairs;;;;)

To see birds fly over the heart
to see water for flowers facing
to see unfixed men standing together
forming opposing words;;;

but this is poetry
The people in the streets are not involved;

& yet sing the isolated garden song; they;
& the lonely mountain;
the dancer whose dance is a distraction;
whose dance is made distracting herself
& me & my songs;itsn yet to really sing.

#21

SORRYX THIS IS IT

You bring me back to the poemx
your movement marks the periphery
I stand upon tonightx Perhaps (counting waxax verbs)

                    the sun will change
                    the beauty of night flowers
                    & the stars I see in you
                    will seem less bright then

but this is no concern of minex

Yes I am disenchanted that I cannot
speak in symbols about whatix
happeningx also ns not loving
what I cannot touchx a vile man
in vile timesx they say of me
this mine is x mirror dark things grown uponit

                    but do not believe Typsiss
                    nor no mark but
                    you is in minex

I is trying to give an apple back
to a laughing Serpent
somewhere in the near Eastx

I don't think hexll be back.

65

<u>You in the morning</u>

You in the morning
I wanted to do you totally more than
every
  in the evening after I can't
  & often I never can as I
  would like to

charge time with love

Origin of something I have never
carried water in

  you confuse me with feelings
    I can't name
    can only affirm

& everybody's a Trojan Horse
filled with tender & vicious weapons
& no openings, no
apparent openings.

#23

HELLO FROM THE SHADOWS
                    xxfor Christopher Walks

of the mind & the universexxx
the mind, its power is in
the substance of
its objects cosmos, or forms** ·
from withoutx structure

x timexresisting thingx
contemplating the altarxs sacred stonex
my life of ceaseless repetitionsx
pointless gesturesx initiate
to the magic power of breath,
of symbolic formxstructures

                    poor product of nature, acting
                    upon what wisdom I havex

I say hello from the shadows
to your passing on the street.

67

CHARACTEROLOGY

       the dominately sacred
       centrexxx merely the navel is the embryo
       of character or personality

This was
the story of The Indian astrologer
       seeking the point
       under the serpents head
       (of the Heavens)
       & it supports the world
       & on that spot
       goes the foundation
       of a temple

But that spot moves
as all things moves
as navel to body moves
as nothing endures without animations
nothing in xxxxxxxx with its goes with
What has gone before; & there's nothing happening
because its happened; Words
force creation consciousness upon us

       XI am Heaven you are EarthXxx
       where's Hell but in our minds?
       Lie down together; let us on the ground.
       as the rains fall, we shall lixy fall
       slaking thirst
       of the ground we lie on

    We justify our excesses
    by the excesses of our goes

       XI will parade
       naked through the streets
       proclaiming the sorcery of the navelXX

Even these actions a participation in what is
sacred at the centre
where I am slowly turning
around a dominately sacred moment of being.

#25

THE LAST TRAIN TO NARCISSUS

                        1
the thing measured you did our things
in an eye stare measure after it was
valued potential for comprehension
noted & after we had turned down
the noise all around
a gentle goodbye fell

                    my lips have formed
                    words for the thing
                    which I will relate one day
                    in songs

Rotten feeling inside
or the slaughtered moments only we are
tears falling we relax

& these words a response or reaction
to a manifestation within
slowly winding out.

69

the struggle remains unseen,
in the darky nobody says
much about it

        ring yourself around
        with roses in the magic
        garunny thorns
        about the navel to protecty
        to cleanse with kisses

Brood on the alternatives
to struggle; weigh the gamble;
the dice may never return, may
for ever roll onxxx

the afternoon falls like passiant's
trousers & i illustrate the dark
for your closing iny

        with my knowledge of thorns

aaept at instinct
i carry your bags aboard that last foolish train.

#26

ALMOST A POEM
                xxfor Robert Hogg

forms are worn away
by recognitionxxthe structures we
have created begin to age,
xxbasically we
extinguish forms
place new forms, new ash
side by side,

vain heads talking
against appearances
of reality, no light
without & no belief
within,

            xI am he who performs
            holy works manifesting
            into form

                    & new men
                    will learn that possession
                    is not an act of creation.x

                        unceasing rehearsal
                        of myth begins
                        each day as does
                        xbxxxxsxx universal combustion myth

Conscious of cyclical
duration I see life
as ritual

                    this is my actual myth,
                    my meaning in behaviour as a last grasp at Being,

Expect no change occurrence,
as best I can explaining,
giving form, the eternal etcetera
sings his song.

71

BOOKS ON IRAN WANTED

or conversations with the hip arab who says
No more prognostications;
peoplex your polis is happening

& it's all therein
this unmentionable

Ten Steps Up Or Down

0*	is of course for	(Aleph)
1*	who makes it happen in context	(Beth)
2*	who changes the context	(Gimel)
3*	who creates my head	(Daleth)
4*	who takes care & reconnoitres	(Heh)
5*	who binds	(Vav)
6*	us as we should be	(Zain)
7*	is power; is consciousness outward	(Sheth)
8*	is power; is consciousness inward	(Teth)
9*	is keeping it hid	(Yod)
10*	is laughing & starting over	(Kaph)

This here is a world of marvels;
Also stern values;

    & these moral things; easily acquired;
      are hard to use

spend a whole life
learning when to say
good or bad
    at the wrong times

& being as lonely as a poet

Give this meaning as you may; or must;
at 5:35 a.m; this 6th day of April; year 1966; the sun rose

for me, for you

You there are no more endings beginning now I want accept them

      (in my dreams women
      are mandalas
      four ins & four outs)

You there is a window with light shining thru & shades just
want stop it

      (around me an order
      occurs I feel
      it fall back into place)

You now its quiet & the clock is ticking out of time
& nothing but vague ideas are suitable giving form away
I breath onto glass & direct traffic in the empty street

      (you don't know what it is
      to have complete control
      over nothing)

So I'll write a song
          about this box & a sleigh
a sleigh & a box
          with no hill
to go down on.

BASELINE VARIATIONS

curiousity

attempts

work

//

same

olaer

m°on

AFTERWORKS II

Ongoing

AFTER BARBARA CARUSO

```
        ONE&
        ON&E
        O&NE
        &ONE

        ONE&
        ON&E
        O&NE
        &ONE

        ONE&
        ON&E
        O&NE
        &ONE

        ONE&
         ON&E
          O&NE
           &ONE

          ONE&
          ON&E
          O&NE
          &ONE

          ONE&
          ON&E
          O&NE
          &ONE

          ONE&
          ON&E
          O&NE
          &ONE

          ONE&
           ON&E
            O&NE
             &ONE
```

Articles of Agreement (Found)

AFTER CIA RINNE

```
words
imparting
the
singular
include
the
plural
and
vice
versa
```

Few Enough Words From How Many (November 26 19)
AFTER LARRY EIGNER

```
each
    colour
        of this                  and
            colour                   each
                                         in
        and                                between
            each
            in
                between
```

I am Trying to Write a Poem

AFTER PHYLLIS WEBB

i.

and **here**

ii.

and here

Little Song

AFTER BILL BISSETT

```
each way, slowly
each way, slowly
each way, slowly
each way, slowly
each way, slowly
each way, slowly
each way, slowly
slowly, each way
slowly, each way
slowly, each way
slowly, each way
slowly, each way
slowly, each way
slowly, each way
```

An Exercise

AFTER LOVISA BULLARD BARNES

youare hewas sawhim didfor letus hearsay

seehow hadbeen fromhope werehere donesoon givemuch

notnow longtime senasome moregoods wellsince toldwhen

thethem thenthey thisthat thesethose theretheir thinkthank

maycan musthave camegone willshall mightcould wouldshould

Essayer

AFTER DANI SPINOSA AND KATE SIKLOSI

Oh my god, make bad art. Make some art that sucks!
                  imperfect
                  sketchy
                  preliminary
                  fundamental
                  central
                  momentous
                  consequential
                  substantial

There is so much beauty to be found in failure.
                                        prodigal
                                        abundant
                                        generous
                                        hospitable
                                        congenial
                                        favourable
                                        encouraging
                                        auspicious

I love this idea of a poem as always kind of, like, a try.
                                                    struggle
                                                    attempt
                                                    experiment
                                                    venture
                                                    essay
                                                    labour
                                                    diligence
                                                    attention
                                                    consideration

But it makes you okay with imperfection. I think that's a
                          incompleteness   good lesson.
                          breach
                          bloom
                          opening
                          aperture
                          puncture
                          rupture
                          tear

An Education

AFTER NICKY DRUMBOLIS

```
letters
letterå
lettełs
lettłeś
letłets
lełełes
lłełeres
letters
łeteres
lełers
letsers
łesters
rstters
setters
letters &
letters
```

Interstitial

AFTER PAUL DUTTON

```
intersticeintersticeintersticeinterstice
  t    i    n    ie     st
    e      nt r ie      s

    e       nt   i      r     e
         ce nt r    e      s

 n e t         s
inters    e        c  t

    t   i e
    t   i  nt
   te st

    er    e
      st     r    e    s        s

    e       nt r   e
       ti e      rs
   t r    e    e s

inter    e    st
  n e st         s

    e  t ce  ter        r    e
intersticeintersticeintersticeinterstice
    (s ic)

 i t
 i    s

 i t
     st e   ers

 i t
       c i te s

 i t
    er         rs

    r    e    s    e  t
    r    e    s    e  t
    r    e    s    e  t

     st e  t
intersticeintersticeintersticeinterstice
```

Winter Landscape

AFTER ROBERT LAX

```
the quiet season  nosaes
    quiet season  nosaes teiuq
          season  nosaes teiuq eht

             eht  the quiet season
       teiuq eht  the quiet
 nosaes teiuq eht  the

the quiet season  nosaes
    quiet season  nosaes teiuq
          season  nosaes teiuq eht
```

Align
AFTER BPNICHOL

along a long enough measure a long lone sound

so what is it--a line a line a line a line a line a line a line
                                               a line
                                               a line
                                               a line
                                               a line
                                               a line
                                               a line
                                               a line
                                               a line
                                               a line
                                               a line
                                               a line
                                               a line
                                               a line
                                               a line
                                               a line
                                               a line
                                               a line
                                               a line
                                               a line
                                               a line
                                               a line
                                               a line
                                               a line
                                               a line
                                               a line
                                               a line
                                               a line
                                               a line
                                               a line
                                               a line
                                               a line
                                               a line
                                               a line
                                               a line
                                               a line
                                               a line
                                               a line
                                               a line
                                               a line
                                               a line
                                               a line
                                               a line

A Moment of Silence (16 08 19)

FOR NELSON BALL

```
if now,
now.

and now,
too.
```

MILOSTNÁ BÁSEŇ

FOR JENN AT 34

In art, you want to stress
some things which you feel
are important. If you eliminate
the things that aren't important
you arrive at the things you
want to say very quickly.

--Norman McLaren

after
years

be

moved

still

be

moved

after
years

after years

be moved

still

be moved

after years

after

years

be

moved

still

after years be moved still

still

be

moved

after

years

still be moved after years

after

years

be

moved

still

be

moved

after

years

after years be moved still be moved after years

                    after
                after years

            after years be
        after years be moved

    after years be moved still be moved after years

                        be moved after years
                        moved after years

                        after years
                        years

SOME AFTERWORDS

"forms are worn away / by recognition"
—WILLIAM HAWKINS, *OTTAWA POEMS* (1966)

This book began following the death of my friend, the poet William Hawkins, on July 4, 2016, when I was gifted his Olivetti Lettera 30 type-writer. The Lettera 30, manufactured in the early 1970s, is a lightweight manual travel typewriter housed in a soft case with a long shoulder strap. I was amazed to discover that the machine had survived! It had been years since there had been a typewriter in the house, and I began re-typing some of Bill's poems on his Olivetti as a way of re-engaging with his work.

I then started to use Bill's Olivetti to explore how my own developing minimalist poetics would be changed if the typewriter was the mode of composition. The result of those explorations—this book—was com-posed entirely on Bill's Olivetti using the same ribbon that was on it when he died (and likely had been for decades). I wanted to explore the con-straints and the freedoms of the typewriter—the ability to feed the same page through the roller repeatedly and the impossibility of doing so in an identical position; the fixed-width type and grid that proved so freeing to poets in the twentieth century; the imperfections of letterforms resulting from wear and tear and the varying pressures of keystrokes; the ability to manipulate the page on different axes; and how the typewriter, through its (typical) use of a standard letter-sized page, places the minimalist work on a large visual field.

All books are full of errors—be they of diction, grammar, technique, fact, bibliography. The typewriter makes visible particular types of error—material errors, machine errors, operator errors. Those errors contrast the dream of precision on which typewriters were advertised; they are a return to the human error from which the typewriter was supposed to offer freedom. They also offer a visual counterpoint to the concision and (presumed) precision of minimalist works.

In the twenty-first century, a book of typewriter works is also neces-sarily a book of decay, and the works in this book are saturated with it. This book documents fragments of keys chipping away over time and type bars becoming warped (the uppercase 'E' and the lower case 'd' in particular caused me problems), components giving out, the scarcity of replacement parts, the loss of knowledge. I have embraced that decay, and while I strove to create clean works, I also "allowed" such imperfections to remain. They register that I typed each sheet on Bill's typewriter.

The majority of the works in this book were imagined and conceived individually over the course of weeks, if not months, prior to my first attempts to create them. This initial thinking often occurred on my walks to and from work. I like the idea of works of only a few words (or less) forming over such long periods of time, particularly as they were created using a machine whose promise of speed drove its adoption. I work slowly at my most productive, and so felt embraced by a process that demanded I slow down even further.

Finally, I have opted to refer to this as a book of typewriter works, conspicuously avoiding terms like concrete, visual, and poem. Despite years of formal study—or perhaps as a result of them—I am not always confident in my ability to delineate between formal categories. I have leaned on the typewriter qualifier for the obvious reason, but also because my interest was in exploring how the typewriter would alter the minimalist work I was already producing, some of which is clearly not concrete or visual, and some of which is perhaps not even poetry. This imprecision does not trouble me, and I hope you feel free to receive these works through any terms you like.

Cameron Anstee
April 2022

NOTES TO THE POEMS

The Larry Eigner epigraph is the entirety of his poem "January 26 78."

The Barbara Caruso epigraph was the first piece in the landmark bpNichol-edited anthology *The Cosmic Chef: An Evening of Concrete* (Ottawa: Oberon Press, 1970).

AFTERWORKS I

This book exists in conversation, directly and indirectly, with past and contemporary typewriter poets, and while I will not hazard to offer an inevitably incomplete list of the works and writers that are in the DNA of this book, the pieces in Afterworks I and Afterworks II, and their respective notes below, offer a partial glimpse of some of the reading and looking and thinking I was doing while working. The two Afterworks sections contain responses to both typewriter works and non-typewriter minimalist works.

"Ellipsis": A response to Heidi Neilson's *Typography of the Period: A Brief Introduction* (New York: [n.p.], 2003). Two ellipses, typed using the uppercase and lowercase periods on my typewriter, have been digitally scanned and enlarged.

"The Golden Ratio": A response to the works of psw.

"Three Raindrops": A response to Mary Ellen Solt's *A Trilogy of Rain* (Urbana: Finial Press, 1970) and "Moon Shot Sonnet" (1964).

"Sheets": A response to the works of Jiří Valoch.

"Evening Spring Sound": A response to Michael Casteels' chapbook *solar-powered light bulb and the lake's achy tooth* (Ottawa: Apt. 9 Press, 2015), a book I had the privilege of publishing.

"An Installation": A response to Alex Porco's *Hear A Window Cry Out* (2020), a series of 101 installations he completed using a light box between March and May 2020.

"The Great Galaxy": A response to Rufino Tamayo's painting of the same name (1979).

"Haiku": A response to LeRoy Gorman's works generally, but also this quotation from Gorman on haiku: "Nothing has been said; rather, into silence the reader enters and is compelled to feel" (LeRoy Gorman, "Outside / Inside: Notes on Visual and Language-Centred Writing in Haiku," *Open Letter* 5.3 [Summer 1982]).

ST. ANDREW VOICES

Primarily a response to Aram Saroyan's *Sled Hill Voices* (London: Goliard Press, 1966), "St. Andrew Voices" was written during the first months spent at home during the COVID-19 pandemic. The Eileen Myles epigraph is from the poem "Transitions" (*Snowflake / different streets* [Seattle: Wave, 2012]).

OTTAWA POEMS

"Ottawa Poems" is a work of erasure. The source text is William Hawkins' *Ottawa Poems*, published by Nelson Ball's Weed/Flower Press in 1966. My erasure was completed by re-typing the entirety of Bill's *Ottawa Poems* on the poet's own typewriter (unfortunately not the one on which he originally wrote the book as this particular Olivetti typewriter dates to the early 1970s, and *Ottawa Poems* was published in 1966). I had completed an earlier version of the erasure via computer during the years I was editing *The Collected Poems of William Hawkins* (Ottawa: Chaudiere Books, 2015), and that version of the series received Bill's blessing. That first version was a way of engaging with Bill's work during the editing of his *Collected Poems*; this second version was a way of returning to his work following his death. A poem from the first version (#26) was published as a POEM broadside by rob mclennan's above/ground press (#336) when the series was under the working title "these actual lines." 3, 7, and 16 from the second version were published in the Canadian issue of *Poemeleon*, also edited by rob mclennan. #17 was published in *These Days*, edited by Jeff Blackman. Selections from the first version of the sequence were also shortlisted for the 2016 John Lent Poetry/Prose Award from Kalamalka Press (Okanagan College).

BASELINE VARIATIONS

Each word in this poem is an individual found work. Errors in alignment are original to the source texts (which, unfortunately, I have lost). Published as a leaflet by St. Andrew Books (Ottawa).

AFTERWORKS II

"Ongoing": A response to Barbara Caruso's presspresspress books, which were produced via rubberstamp, not typewriter, but offer one of the most thoughtful explorations of the making of small works and small books in Canadian small press.

"Articles of Agreement": A response to Cia Rinne's *zaroum* (Helsinki: [n.p.], 2001) and *Notes for Soloists* (Stockholm: OEI Editör, 2009). A non-typewriter version of this poem was published in a Canadian issue of *The Café Review* (Spring 2019) edited by Robert Hogg.

"Few Enough Words from How Many": The title is taken from the essay "Dilemmas By Their Horns" by Larry Eigner (*areas lights heights* [New York: Roof Books, 1989]). This poem was published as a broadside by Happy Monks Press (2020).

"I am Trying to Write a Poem": A response to Phyllis Webb's *Naked Poems* (Vancouver: Periwinkle Press, 1965).

"Little Song": A response to bill bissett's typewriter work generally, and to the book *Liberating Skies* (Vancouver: blewointment press, 1969) specifically. Published in *Peter F. Yacht Club*, edited by rob mclennan. A non-typewriter version of this poem was published in a Canadian issue of *The Café Review* (Spring 2019) edited by Robert Hogg.

"An Exercise": This is an exercise in Lovisa Bullard Barnes' *How to Become an Expert in Typewriting: A Complete Instructor Designed Especially for the Remington* (St. Louis: [n.p.], 1890) and was completed blind, via touch-typing, in a single attempt. Lovisa Bullard Barnes unintentionally marks the confluence of art and commerce contained in the typewriter when she implores the student of the typewriter to "write every sentence as thought it were to be put on exhibition [...]. Make all your writing as perfect as though it were to be paid for."

"Essayer": A response to a discussion between Dani Spinosa and Kate Siklosi, published in Spinosa's *OO: Typewriter Poems* (Halifax and Prince Edward County: Invisible Publishing, 2020). Prompted by Spinosa's exploration of the glosa in *OO*, this work takes four lines directly from the conversation (two each from Spinosa and Siklosi), and traces a path through a thesaurus beginning with one word in each line.

"An Education": A response to the bookselling career—what an inadequate description!—of Nicky Drumbolis, one of the great caretakers of the small press in Canada.

"Interstitial": A response to "Solitude" by Paul Dutton.

"A Winter Landscape": A response to the works of Robert Lax.

"Align": A response to the works and influence of bpNichol.

"A Moment of Silence": Written on August 16, 2019, the day of Nelson Ball's death. I published this poem as a rubber-stamped postcard in Fall 2019.

MILOSTNÁ BÁSEŇ

This poem was prepared in an edition of one as a birthday present for my partner, Jenn. "Milostná Báseň" is a Google-generated translation of "Love Poem" into Czech. The Norman McLaren epigraph is quoted from the book *Norman McLaren on the Creative Process* (National Film Board of Canada, 1991), and the poem responds to McLaren's approach to animation and filmmaking.

ACKNOWLEDGEMENTS

Thank you to the incomparable Invisible Publishing team, present and past—Norm Nehmetallah, Leigh Nash, Andrew Faulkner, Megan Fildes, Julie Wilson—for taking on this manuscript and for turning it into this book.

Thank you to my editor, derek beaulieu, for your keen and encouraging editorial eye, and for bearing with me.

Thank you to William Hawkins (and to Peter Bowie) for friendship, for poems, and for your Olivetti Lettera 30.

Thank you to folks who supported this manuscript at different stages in different ways: my parents, Jeff Blackman, Michael Casteels, Peter Gibbon, Susan Holbrook, Zane Koss, Justin Million, Stuart Ross, Aram Saroyan, Kate Siklosi, Dani Spinosa.

Thank you to editors who published excerpts from this book. Thank you to the Ontario Arts Council for Recommender Grants that supported the production of this work.

Thank you, finally, to my partner Jenn (and to our cats) for continuing to support my writing regardless of how strange it gets, for your questions and encouragement throughout this and other projects, and for a love and a life that make space for all this.

INVISIBLE PUBLISHING produces fine Canadian literature for those who enjoy such things. As an independent, not-for-profit publisher, our work includes building communities that sustain and encourage engaging, literary, and current writing.

Invisible Publishing has been in operation for over a decade. We released our first fiction titles in the spring of 2007, and our catalogue has come to include works of graphic fiction and nonfiction, pop culture biographies, experimental poetry, and prose.

We are committed to publishing diverse voices and experiences. In acknowledging historical and systemic barriers, and the limits of our existing catalogue, we strongly encourage writers from LGBTQ2SIA+ communities, Indigenous writers, and writers of colour to submit their work.

Invisible Publishing is also home to the Bibliophonic series of music books and the Throwback series of CanLit reissues.

If you'd like to know more, please get in touch:
info@invisiblepublishing.com